TRAINED TO FAIL

DEDICATIONS

I am dedicating this book to a wonderful, loving woman. My wife Karen. Without her my book would not even be possible. Also, I am dedicating my book to my three sons, Tyrone, Vincent and A.J. I am so proud of them.

ACKNOWLEDGEMENTS

Imani Lacy
Victoria Lacy
Teneecia Brannon
Monroe Lacy, Jr.
Marc Henderson
Dwight Maynor
Todd Haskins
Darren Brooks
Thank you for always being real with me. Thank you for hanging in there with me through thick and thin.

TABLE OF CONTENTS

<u>INTRODUCTION</u>

From the beginning of time since birth, women have been trained to seek out and look for a good mate by looking at what material accomplishments he has. Even by looking at what status he has. Little girls for so many years have been taught that the more a man has to offer them, the better he would be as a husband. By the same token, men have been taught that women will be looking for all these things. Thus, we have men for one reason or another that uses their material accomplishments as a manipulation tool to have their way with sometimes vulnerable, naïve, and possibly, misguided women. Let's get this fact out of the way early. Some men are horrible, narcissistic, selfish men. That is a fact that cannot be disputed, but what I am going to try to do with this book is try and help women see why women fail with men. Because women do have a part in this ongoing issue of successful relationships.

CHAPTER ONE

KIESHA

There is this woman named Kiesha. She was born into a large family. She had several sisters and several brothers. Kiesha grew up craving attention, due to the fact that she was on the latter end of a large family. Kiesha was a pretty good kid growing up. She for a short while had both of her parents.

But, unfortunately one day Kiesha's mom left her father. The sad thing is, that no one that knew the man could understand why Kiesha's mom would just up and leave Kiesha's father. Kiesha's father was actually liked by more people than her mom.

Kiesha's mom was known for being surly and selfish. But Kiesha's father was known to be a kind, generous and a giving man. Well, Keisha's mom separated the family.

Keisha's mom not only separated the family, but because of her selfishness, decided to make it hard for Kiesha's father to be able to visit his children that remained at home. So Keisha had to grow up without her father being around until she was able to become old enough to go and visit her father on her own. Kiesha's mother in many peoples eyes, never really had a reason to leave her father, but Kiesha's mother over the years told many different stories to her children trying to justify her leaving. However, Kiesha's father never bad mouthed Kiesha's mother to his children.

Kiesha grew up to have interest in young men. Kiesha had casual dates along the way while in high school. Kiesha realizes though that these guys intentions are selfish, she realized that all these guys that she was trying to get to know was only after her virginity!

Keisha had managed to maintain her

virginity late up into her later years of high school. All the young men knew it because Kiesha's friends that were not virgins told everyone that Kiesha was still a virgin. Wow! Thirty years ago it would not be so surprising that a young lady had maintained her virginity.

What was even more remarkable about Kiesha keeping her virginity was the fact that Kiesha's mother did not have an open dialogue with her children. The only thing Kiesha's mother would ever show concern about was money!

So if they wanted to talk about earning

money, Kiesha's mother was always ready to talk about that. The funny thing is Kiesha's mother never earned much money of her own. So when the time came for Kiesha to choose a serious companion she had no one to discuss possible red flags, things she probably should have avoided. Because of having the same example of a mother, none of her siblings could be of any assistance because all of them had been through numerous failed relationships.

You see how much parents examples in life can influence a person's life. So this guy came along that had developed into an expert at telling women what they wanted to hear.

Oh, back to Kiesha's mother, if a guy had a good job or was well-off, Kiesha's mother did not care about what kind of person he was. So her advice to Kiesha was if he has a good job or is well-off you can work with that!

So as you can see Kiesha's mother was the vessel which by Kiesha was brought into this world, but she can't really be considered a mother. Because the instructing, compassion, nurturing, caring and love was never given to Kiesha from her mother. Now ask yourself how was Kiesha suppose to be prepared for what life in general would throw at her, let alone bring in romantic relationships? Just writing this saddens me! How can anyone be prepared for the world when you don't get the needed love, training, and nurturing that even a mother of little means is capable of giving?

Okay, now that your still trying to get your mind to comprehend how could a mother be so self-absorbed in herself. Kiesha now turns seventeen and Kiesha's mother puts her out of the house while she is still in high school.

Like I told you at the beginning of this story, Kiesha was a good person and she never got in trouble. She never talked back. Kiesha's mom was not buying school supplies nor school clothes. So the little job that Kiesha had she had to buy herself some things for school. Kiesha's mother, however, felt that Kiesha should be giving all her check to her mom. So Kiesha's mom put Kiesha out; still in high school.

Kiesha was able to stay with her older sister, but Kiesha became depressed because she felt abandoned. She would cry often when she would think of how her mother did her. She could not understand how this could happen to her.

Now can you imagine what happened next while in this vulnerable state? Yes, she met this guy. Having a severe need to feel wanted and worthy, Kiesha wanted to feel loved.

Kiesha was not in a position to pay attention to the warning signs. So she began her first real relationship with a young man that was very unstable. This young man was insecure and had a lot of insecurities within himself. But, Kiesha had been abandoned and she had an extreme fear of being abandoned again. Kiesha overlooked things that would have made other women run!

Kiesha did not have any idea of how a healthy relationship should be. So a lot of the things that were going on, Kiesha kind of thought that was just how it is suppose to be. Kiesha ended up suffering a lot of verbal and physical abuse. And because Kiesha had shared the misfortunes of not getting the instruction, training, nurturing and love growing up, with this guy, he used it against her to get her to stay longer. He would convince her that everyone just wanted to break them up. So sad! So sad!

Finally it was just too much that Kiesha was taking, but it was the guy that really left. Now you would think that Kiesha would learn from that bad experience. But what ended up happening was it caused Kiesha to have a deeper need to feel worthy and the need to feel wanted.

Due to more bad advice and, bad examples from older siblings, Kiesha began to be conditioned to believe that there are just some things you are going to have to except from men.

Kiesha began a dangerous journey of dating and sleeping with more and more men, but none of these men ever really cared about Kiesha. Kiesha even began to convince herself that all these men were just friends. Friends with benefits, but none of these men considered Kiesha a friend. All of these men just considered Kiesha easy. Some even titled her or nicknamed her "The Old Standby." Some of the men would joke that all I got to do is buy her dinner and a couple of drinks. But the sad thing is that it was making Kiesha feel worthy because she felt like if a man was willing to have sex with her, then she has to have some value. But some men will have sex with anyone that will lay down with them.

Kiesha began to go through these cycles

where she will one month say she did not need a man. Then two months later she would say she want to get married and would get very emotional about it. Then the summer block buster movie would come out putting men down and then she would be back on that, "I don't need a man" cycle. All the while she is dating off and on. She dates men that supposedly have left their babies mommas or wives.

The bad cycle where the men end up going back to their mates after Kiesha has given herself to these men for months. The sad thing is that Kiesha and her sisters continue the same cycle over and over again. They date the same type of man over and over again. Even when they think they are picking a different kind of guy.

There is this one man that Kiesha has expressed an interest in being willing to date, or even marry. The sad thing is that this guy has said that Kiesha is a nice person, but he just can't get past her reputation of sleeping with so many men in the past. The sad thing is that Kiesha has convinced herself into believing she has not slept with a lot of men, but Kiesha knows the truth. That is why she have said that she is going to have to leave this town, because this town is too small. This town could be large as she want it to be. Until Kiesha changes some things about herself, things are not going to get better.

Her first change need to be, stop following the advice of people that are in the same situation that she is in. Second, Kiesha need to stand on her own and do things on her own. Third, Kiesha need to learn how to love herself and learn to require better treatment. Fourth, Kiesha must stop thinking that her sexual abilities will make a man act right. If the man is a dog he is going to remain a dog. A better word would be a pig because pigs eat everything even its own feces.

Fifth, Kiesha has to become respectful of her mate when he is with her and when he is not around, because no man wants to marry a flirt. There is no way you can justify flirting with another man. Kiesha will deny it, but I have seen Kiesha flirt with other guys right in front of the man she was dating, behind his back. That is a trait that Kiesha picked up from one of her older sisters.

Sixth, Kiesha must start to except

responsibility for some of her reputation because if she does not then she will never be able to fix her reputation. Seventh, realize that she does need to fix her reputation, because your reputation in life is just as important as your credit.

WARNING SIGNS THAT WOMEN OVERLOOK

1. When your man treat your sister or your female cousin better than you.

2. When at family functions your man attention is on your sister or female cousin for most of the event.

3. He gives other women compliments all the time, but hardly ever give you any.

4. When your man care more about what he wants, than what you want.

5. When your man keep using his past to stop you and him from moving forward, in his and your future. Because if that woman from the past ever wants him back, she can get him back secretly.

6. When the man you are interested in pays more than necessary attention to his personal grooming.

7. When your man has no sense of common responsibility.

8. When your man is always making subtle put-downs.

9. When your man can never admit wrong or apologize.

10. When your man is completely disrespectful to his mother.

CHAPTER TWO

SUSAN

Susan is a woman that on the surface, would appear to have had it all. Susan was in a long term relationship. Susan was married to a professional baseball player, that traveled all over the world. Susan was taken along with her husband to many parts of the world. Susan's husband was not rich, but he earned six figure salaries each year.

It came to a point where Susan began to not want to go with her husband any longer on his jobs overseas. Susan's husband would be gone for four to six months at a time. We all know how long distance relationships work, but usually they don't work out.

Now Susan would begin to stay home instead of going with her husband. Susan's husband would send just about all his money home to his wife, with the hope that Susan was taking care of business. Susan however did a little for the house with the money, but also spent a lot of unnecessary money.

Susan comes from a large family. Susan would spend a lot of money on her family over the years, that her husband did not know about. Susan would also began to go out to clubs with some of her girlfriends and sisters, while her husband was gone. Susan's husband would hear about this by way of his family, but Susan was so manipulative that she would convince her husband that she was not doing all what his family was saying about her. She would say things like you know your family does not like me! But because she was right, her husband was lolled into believing her. Now doesn't that sound familiar. Sound like the same thing men say to women when they get told on. So Susan's partying without her husband continued.

After the end of Susan's husband contracts,

at the end of each season he would come home. As time went by it became harder and longer for Susan's husband to get a job. So the long laps in time began to cause arguments between Susan and her husband.

Susan's husband began to notice that as long as the money was right, Susan showed him and gave him the utmost respect. But when his money was running short, the more Susan did not care about showing him respect. Susan's husband was still able to get contracts, but they just took longer to come by.

All of sudden because Susan was seeing the

end of her husband's professional career come to an end, she now began to see all kinds of things she did not like about her husband. Susan began to have rumors developing about her. That she had been cheating on her husband for years.

Susan was rumored to have multiple extra affairs. Susan's husband loved her so much that he forced himself to ignore all the rumors. Susan's husband began to try harder to make Susan love him more, and love him only!

The sad thing was that a good woman would have appreciated her husband ignoring the rumors and working hard to gain her love, but not Susan. She took that as a sign of weakness and it caused her to do him worse. His career came to an end like all athletes. Like I told you before he did okay, but he was not rich. Susan never developed anything out of herself, but every year spent more and more money. It left their family broke. Now everything began to hit the fan. More rumors of Susan's infidelity began to boil over. The money was gone, so all respect for her husband went out the window. So Susan started going out to parties even though her husband was at home. Susan sometimes would lie and say she was going to do something else or to help a friend, but really Susan was going to Army Base parties, house parties, and so on.

One sad day came when Susan fell in love with a boy! I say boy because he was so much younger than her. Susan had went so far as to think about leaving her family to be with this boy. Susan did not care. She even told her husband that she was going to leave with this boy. You probably are wondering how can any person be so uncaring. Well, Susan had seen how easy her mother left her father for no apparent reason, although some will argue that this have nothing to do with Susan's situation.

Let me share this with you. Susan comes from a family of twelve siblings. None of her siblings have had a successful marriage. Every last one of them have failed and have gotten divorces. Some of them have been divorced two times. For some reason their family lack the ability to make their mates feel loved. Lack the ability to love. Some of them don't know what love is. One of Susan's siblings stated that she can never remember her mother ever telling their father that she loved him. And don't even remember seeing her mother hug their father. Sad isn't it!

Well back to Susan - Susan for one reason or another ended up staying with her husband this time. After making him go through so much emotional torture of losing his wife to a younger man. Pushing her husband to the point of crying like a baby and having him beg her not leave him, she stayed.

Things were not good though. Susan always had control of the relationship because she really did not give a damn whether or not if they stayed together. But Susan's husband wanted her and his family to stay together dearly. You see when only one person really cares than it's just a matter of time! Just a matter of time before it's all over! Because the person that's doing all the caring and loving will one day snap and either become dangerous or develop enough strength to start caring about themselves. Then that person due to years of feeling unloved, uncared for and feeling like the only thing wrong with their mate is pure selfishness or that they just don't possess the human ability to express love, will begin to develop animosity or hate for their mate.

Back to Susan - Susan continued to live with her husband for awhile longer. At many get-togethers, Susan and her husband would go overboard to prove to other people that they were in love, but everyone that was close to Susan knew it was all fake. In fact, Susan's sisters would talk about how it was not real when Susan was not around. They knew what Susan was into because often they were with Susan when she was doing things.

The toll of not having a lot of money anymore took it's toll on this relationship, because this relationship had began about money and it ended about money. Susan ended up leaving her husband. Susan's reasons for leaving her husband was ironic, because Susan's complaint was that her husband and family did not respect her and that she felt disrespected in her own house. Ironic because this is what Susan had done to her family in secret for many years. Disrespect her family!

Susan left her husband and moved in with a man that she had been rumored to been having an affair with early in her marriage. She moved in with him the same day she left her husband.

Things Susan need to change - first, Susan need to stop wanting to be the center of attention everywhere she goes. Second, Susan need to change her self-centeredness. Third, Susan need to be honest with herself and start trying to work toward correcting what mistakes she have made. Make amends and stop playing the victim because she is being seen in a bad light. Fourth, allow herself to feel wrong and remorseful. Fifth, stop trying to justify. Sixth, learn how to love. How to show love. How to express love. Seventh, learn what love is and not depend on what she saw growing up in her household as a child.

CHAPTER THREE

<u>KIM</u>

Kim is a woman that is a little out the ordinary. Kim most of her adult life has remained in dysfunctional relationships. Kim's choices in men has had a serious affect on her children's development. You see Kim chose a man that has always been mentally unstable. Kim through the years have always been bullheaded.

When Kim was a little girl it was said that she had a stubbornness to her that often caused riffs between her and her mother. At one point in Kim's life, Kim and her mother finally came to a point where she told her mother that she did not want the religion that her mother had tried to bring Kim and the rest of Kim's siblings up in. So some say that Kim chose this one guy to get involved with in an attempt to get out of the house faster.

Like I told you before, this guy and his family was known to be unstable, but due to Kim's stubbornness and desperation she could not, or refuse to pay attention to the warning signs. Also, my friends, after you finish reading about Kim I will let you be the judge, if maybe Kim herself came into this relationship unstable, but back to Kim.

So Kim began to live with this man. This is a relationship I would not wish on no one, rather or not if you are a woman or a man. Early into the relationship, Kim and her mate began to have violent fights. Kim's mate was very insecure. Every time Kim turned around she was always being accused of cheating. Also, Kim's mate began to display a violent temper whenever he would drink alcohol.

Whenever Kim's mate would drink, he would start to think everyone in the room was talking about him. He ruined many fun gatherings with his paranoia and mental instability. Every time he would drink at gatherings, it became a custom for some of the family to began to leave the party whenever they would see this guy beginning to drink.

Now that is a shame that people would actually keep an eye on this guy at the party, because they wanted to make sure they left as soon as he started drinking. Kim's mate would go through the same cycle every single time he drunk. First, he would start off happy. Next, he would get quite. Then he would start to look at people every time they laughed. Even if the person laughing was in a totally different room, in a different conversation. Then he would begin to mumble things up under his breath to himself. Slowly but surely, his mumbling would turn into outbursts. It was almost as if he was hearing voices inside his head. People got so tired of this happening at every party, or get-together, at functions that were suppose to be fun and happy.

This mentally disturbed man would eventually want to fight someone at the party. I mean this was every time. But then out of no where, every time Kim's mate would go through a period of remorse and start to cry. He would then start to apologize to everyone, but this became a broken record.

Kim, however, never stressed or was embarrassed by her mate's behavior. This was done over and over in front of Kim and her mate's children. It happened so much that even the children became desensitized to this behavior. Of course with this behavior going on, Kim and her mate would get into physical fights a lot over the years. All in front of their children. It is no wonder their daughter ended up getting involved with a man just like her father.

It is so true how what a kid sees growing up,

will have a profound affect on their emotional and overall development. Because like I stated before, Kim's oldest daughter has gotten involved with a man that displays a lot of the characteristics of her father. This man has so many different kids by so many different women. Kim's daughter is well aware of this, but yet she is still drawn to this man. Kim's oldest son is drawn to women just like Kim, his mother.

You see Kim is kind of hard to describe, but I will try. Kim is indifferent about everything. You can do something extremely nice for Kim and her demeanor would be the same as if you had did something extremely mean to Kim. Things that the average person would be worried about, Kim visibly never show any concern.

Kim, even when her children was separated from her for awhile, due to herself and her mate never having any stability in their life, never displayed any stress or pain over being separated from her children. Some of her children had to stay with other relatives due to Kim being evicted, but you would never know it by Kim's everyday demeanor. It seemed like it was no issue at all going on in her life. Even when Kim was fighting with her mate, even her aggression still was emotionless.

So this is the kind of woman that Kim's son had developed an attraction to. Kim continued to be with her mate off and on for years. Also, Kim continued to have kids over the years. Kim's father asked Kim why does she continue to have children by this man if she did not love this man? Because Kim was always being heard saying that she does not love this man. But she ended up having six kids by this man.

Finally, Kim and her mate split up for good because Kim started messing around with the next door neighbor. This guy was suppose to have been friends with Kim's long term mate, but what was even worse was that this neighbor was married. Kim, however, was indifferent to this fact. Kim allowed herself to be demeaned by the fact that this guy would only hang out with Kim after dark. Also, this guy would make Kim pay for all the hotel hookups.

The sad thing too was that Kim was spending her money on this guy that was married. But she had a son that was in high school that needed Kim to be spending that money on him. Kim worked crazy hours, rotating shifts, but whenever Kim did have time off she would wait around and grovel over the little time that the married man would give her.

While Kim's son that played high school sports would never see his mother, Kim at any of his games. That young man was a super star, but he never felt the support of his mother. She always had excuses and her siblings tended to help her come up with excuses.

It had gotten so bad between Kim and her son that Kim's son moved in with another family that showed him more love than his own mother. Once again Kim was indifferent.

Now the only time Kim would attempt to show any emotions about her son's decision to move in with another family was when she was around her siblings and her mother. But only if they would inquire if she was okay with it or if they would say how could you let someone else take care of your son. That was the only time Kim would act like she was sadden by it, but she would never do anything to fix the situation.

Kim continued to be a sperm trash receptacle for a married man. Until one day the married man decided that he had enough of the extras on the side he was getting with Kim. Now you would think how much worse could it get with Kim. But that son that Kim was neglecting for a married man, it has been rumored for years that Kim is letting that young man believe that his father is her longtime mate. But a lot of people even Kim's longtime mate no longer believes it to be true. But this too Kim is indifferent about. How selfish can one person be! Where did Kim learn such selfishness? The son does not even believe the man that he was told is his father, is actually his father.

If Kim had any decency in her and is not actually mentally delayed, don't you think for her son's sake she would at least try to prove that her longtime mate is the father or tell her son who his real father is!

Things that Kim needs in order to change or improve her life: First, Kim needs a psychological evaluation because in Kim's family her mother always tried to hide any potential mental problems that her children might have. Instead of getting them the proper treatment that they might need. Because Kim's mother was ashamed and embarrassed to admit that something could be wrong with her kids. I guess we now know where Kim got or learned selfishness.

Second, once Kim receives the medical mental evaluation, Kim should follow-up with the recommendations.

Third, Kim should reach out to her children and apologize to them for taking them through hell in their childhood, and help her kids to see how she is getting help. Then try to be a better grandparent than she was as a parent. If her children will listen, help them to see how what she put them through growing up could be affecting their decision-making in their life.

If Kim does these things it will help her to

get in tune with herself and put her on track

toward a happier life. Whereby, she will become

emotionally and spiritually well-rounded.

CHAPTER FOUR

TANYA

Tanya is a woman that a lot of her problems have a direct correlation to the way her mother treated her, or what her mother did not give her growing up. Tanya is a woman that is always in need of approval due to the fact that although being one of the oldest, her mother never gave her the seal or stamp of approval that she gave a much younger sibling of Tanya's. The praise that little girls thrive on from their mothers. The same old that-a-boy, that little boys crave from their fathers.

You see Tanya never got that from her

mother growing up, instead she always got...

"look what your sister is doing, look how pretty she is." Tanya's mother would always brag on Tanya's little sister at every function or event where people would mingle. Everyone could see how proud Tanya's mother was of Tanya's little sister. It was so bad that you would have thought that this woman only had the little sister.

So Tanya grew up constantly seeking her mother's attention and approval. Over the years Tanya would try to convince herself that she did not need it, but she never was able to convince herself. Also Tanya tried to reason with herself that maybe my mother realizes that in order for my little sister to survive in this world, my mother had to give her all the praise. That would help Tanya for awhile, but she would eventually feel depressed again about it.

Tanya eventually became of age that she was interested in guys. Tanya at this age was already tired of her mother knowingly or unknowingly showing favoritism toward her younger sister. That when Tanya's mother would say something about guys, Tanya was not trying to hear it. Tanya's mother was heard many times over the years saying that Tanya's little sister was the most like her of all her children. Can you imagine hearing this come from your mother over and over, throughout the years. It's almost as if Tanya's mother was saying if she could go back in time and only have one, it would be Tanya's little sister and that's all. So you can see why Tanya's life has been full of approval seeking. Because of this Tanya was susceptible to men that were able to pick up on that Tanya wants approval.

Tanya's first husband was that smooth talking guy, that told Tanya whatever she wanted to hear. He had an exceptional skill of telling

Tanya what she needed to hear, but just like anything when it's not real or sincere then it will not last. Although Tanya continued to love her husband, his feeling begin to change as Tanya began to gain weight. You see this man had always really been about himself.

In the beginning Tanya's husband was so self-centered that his interest in Tanya was solely a big game to him. Because his little click that he ran with, all felt that they were the best things that could have ever happened to women. His entire click felt like any woman that they pursued should be thanking God that they even chose them. But of course Tanya could not see the warning signs that her future husband would always care only about himself. He would only care about what is best for him. He would always care about how he looked to his boy.

You see Tanya's mother while Tanya was growing up has always shown a high regard for material possessions. Also, Tanya's mother has visibly shown a deep respect for men that have been in possession of much materially. Tanya's first husband in the beginning would talk about what all he planned to acquire materially. The influence of her mother growing up made it hard for Tanya to pay attention to any warning signs about this guy. This guy was always in competition with his friends. Just like the beginning of Tanya and his relationship.

He had a bet with his click of friends over who was going to get Tanya as a wife. Tanya found out about it later into the marriage, but you wonder if she would have known before would she still have married him. Well, she did marry him and as time went on in the marriage, he still made their marriage a competition between him and his friends. He wanted Tanya to always look better than any of his friends wives. You could just imagine if she gained a little weight.　　He would, in the beginning, try to make it seem like he was doing it for her by turning it into a "guess what"? competition. He would tell Tanya that if she lost all the weight then he would take her on a shopping spree. That seems harmless right? But when that stop working he began to distance himself physically. She became an embarrassment to him.

You see his selfishness finally took over the arrangement because that is all it ever was, just an arrangement until someone violate the spoken or unspoken rule. The rule that had been broken was that Tanya had not kept herself as the ideal trophy wife. Tanya's husband went out and found what he though would compliment his image again. This started Tanya on a downward spiral.

Tanya had no kind of credible support. No good advice that would help Tanya from spiraling into a depressive state, where Tanya would begin to make chronic mistakes in her life decisions. Tanya was rumored to have fallen in love with a street pharmacists. Tanya became so desperate that when one of her brothers brought this guy around to introduce one of her younger sisters to, she pursued this guy. This guy did not even want Tanya, but because of Tanya's desperation as well as living in a depressed state, she literally threw herself at this man. Of course, since her younger sister was not interested in this guy, he went ahead and took what Tanya was throwing at him. This guy carried himself like he had it all together.

To make a long story short this guy obliged himself of what Tanya was giving away for free, with no strings attached. Tanya's romantic life had gone to hell in a hand basket! Yet she felt the need to try and advise her younger sisters on who they should try to get to know. When she had found out that one of her younger sisters had fallen in love with a guy. Tanya had the audacity to tell her little sister that she should get to know some other guys before she choose to marry that guy. But Tanya's meaning of get to know other guys was to have sex with other guys, before she choose to only have sex with just one for the rest of her life. Fortunately, Tanya's little sister did not listen to her, and take her advice. Tanya continued to spiral downward, deeper and deeper into a depressive, desperate state.

It was rumored that Tanya even

experimented in a relationship with another woman for awhile. That would not be surprising because Tanya began to make statements like, "I don't need a man"!, but then a few months would go by and she would be heard saying she wanted a man. She was always on mental rollercoaster.

You would think that Tanya had been through enough and that she would take some steps to try to change the way things were going in her life. Whether or not if she went to a therapist or looked to religion to change. Sadly though, the way Tanya's life was going downward mirrored the way her mother's life spiraled downward after her divorce from Tanya's father. The quality of men drastically deteriorated and the type of man chosen by Tanya's mother was what Tanya seem to be following in her life.

Tanya's second husband was a snake. Talk about lies! This guy lied so much that he did not know when he was lying. This second husband was just no good. He was just a walking travesty, but of course, Tanya could not see it.

This guy came into Tanya's life and it went from bad to worst quickly. This man was promising this and promising that. All on a short order cooks salary. He promised to have brand new carpet put in Tanya's house from wall to wall.

This guy ended up getting Tanya fired from a long time job. Tanya ended up losing her house that she had long before this guy came around. This guy really took Tanya down fast. It was even rumored that this guy had got Tanya hooked on drugs. It was rumored that he got Tanya to use it to help her lose weight.

This guy was very manipulative. This guy got Tanya to move away from her family. About two hours and thirty minutes. Once he got her that far away from all her family, he became even worse. He begin to verbally abuse Tanya. He did such a good job mentally on Tanya that when the day came for Tanya to finally leave this guy because of something this guy had done, that was unforgivable.

Still Tanya did not want to let go of this guy. This guy finally left due to the fallout that he was facing from Tanya's family. Tanya kind of went into a depression after this guy left because no matter what this guy had done, she did not really want to leave him. This would prove to be

Tanya's second divorce.

Now you would have thought that it could not get any worse for Tanya, but it did. Tanya some kind of way met this guy that had been in and out of prison. Now this guy had a Ph.D. in manipulation. This guy was known to have kids all over town by several different baby mamas. This guy was so good at reading what Tanya needed to hear. He knew just what to tell her. Tanya, by this time in her life she just wanted someone.

Now this guy would do little things for Tanya, but you best believe that this guy got ten times more out of Tanya than he ever gave her. Tanya had a habit of picking guys that she was scared of so in some ways even if Tanya would see some signs that maybe she should not remain with the guy, she would be too intimidated to call off the relationship. Fortunately, for Tanya with this guy when the industry that Tanya was working in went under and Tanya's income crumbled, this guy moved on because he no longer saw Tanya as an asset. Tanya seems to keep falling for these types of men.

What Tanya needs to do to keep from

continuing in her cycle: First, Tanya needs to stop looking at the façade that manipulative men give off. Second, Tanya has to get back to what she knows is right. What she was taught growing up. She need to look for a mate that has the same belief system that she once had. As long as she keeps looking for someone without it, she will never find a mate that truly loves her for better or for worse.

WHAT GOOD MEN WANT IN A COMPANION

A. To feel really loved.

B. To feel wanted.

C. To feel respected above any other man.

D. To feel understood.

E. To feel desired and craved.

F. To feel represented or respected even when he   is not around.

G. To feel supported.

H. Wants to make love/have sex on a regular basis (sex is not everything in a relationship, but it is important in a relationship.

CHAPTER FIVE

<u>TINA</u>

Tina is a woman that has very low self-esteem. She has insecurities about her appearance. Tina has a long history of developing feelings for those that have shown her some kindness. Tina was rumored to, after meeting a guy the same day, have sex with them. Tina over the years developed a control issue.

Tina developed a need to control the man she was with. Tina, although she finally came across a man that she could control, however, seem to be drawn and attracted to men that she could not control. Tina once developed an

attraction for another man although she had been
living with her live-in boyfriend for over eight
years.

Although Tina and her live-in boyfriend had
four kids, Tina was rumored to have many
infidelities. Some, her live-in boyfriend found
out about it. Some he did not. At one point, Tina
met a guy that was very dominating! Tina ended
up leaving her live-in boyfriend for this guy for
a little while. Something else that drew Tina to
this guy was the flair and flash that this guy
perpetrated. The day that Tina and this guy met,
it was rumored that she was on her monthly

cycle, so she was unable to have sex with him. Tina was rumored to voluntarily give him oral sex, but after about a month of being with this guy, the guy had the nerve to call up Tina's live-in boyfriend, and proceeded to tell him that he was done with Tina. He then said that he was sending her back to him. Well, the live-in boyfriend took Tina back saying that it was for the kids benefit, but really he loved Tina. So when Tina came back, of course, she made sure she came back controlling the entire situation.

Tina would not answer any questions that her live-in boyfriend would ask, regarding what all she had done with the guy she had left her boyfriend for. The one question that Tina's boyfriend wanted answered was something the guy had told him. The guy had told him that he should not take her back, because she had cheated with someone close to him. Someone related to him, but Tina would never answer him.

Tina had always dominated this relationship. Tina knew that her boyfriend loved her so much, that he would accept her back any way. So he took her back. Of course, many more situations came about where Tina developed feelings for men that would not bow down to her.

The sad thing is that although Tina's boyfriend knew Tina's past history, he always was mad at the guys, even though Tina would always be the pursuer. Many times guys would tell Tina "NO" out of respect for her boyfriend, but Tina would pursue even harder. Tina was willing to do things for other men that she was drawn to, that she would not do for her boyfriend. So you know now how this relationship eventually turned out. Tina left him again for someone she could not control.

What could Tina do to make things better in

her life. To be honest, I do not know what would help her make her life better, because Tina is never satisfied. Tina gets bored quickly, so Tina will continue to seek something new.

CHAPTER SIX

DONNA

Donna is a woman that loves attention. She loves attention so much, it is often to her demise. Donna grew up in an environment without positive role models. In fact, Donna's father was known to be a street pimp. It is unknown for sure if Donna's mother was one of her father's prostitutes, but because of this environment that Donna have grown up in, it has put her on a road of subconsciously seeking men just like her father. They may not be pimps like her father, but they are very manipulative. They are very good at saying what women want to hear.

What is also sad about Donna's situation is that her aunts are of no help. They tell Donna that men will be men. They have Donna feeling like she should just get use to her man cheating on her. That it is just a fact of life, that all men eventually cheat.

Donna have been cheated on by every man that she has been with so she have come to believe her aunts. Donna's first husband cheated with any women that would have him, but all the while he was constantly accusing Donna of cheating. He would constantly work on tearing down Donna's self-esteem. Donna's husband was African American and Philippino so to a lot of women he is very attractive. He even cheated with women in the same apartments that he and Donna lived in.

For months he would tell Donna that he was just hanging out at a friend of his in the apartments that they lived in, playing video games. Donna complained many times to him that it does not look right for him to be staying all night at someone else house, when he has a wife. He kept making up excuses and accused Donna of just being insecure. But all the while he had a home wrecker that did not care that he had a wife. All she was concerned with was that he make sure that he gives her quality time.

He ended up getting that woman and Donna pregnant at the same time. It is thought that he purposely got Donna pregnant after he realized that the home wrecker was already pregnant. He did that in order to have something to hold onto Donna with, once she found out about the other woman. Well it worked!

Donna did not want her second child to have to grow up without it's father. Donna already had a daughter growing up without her father, because he had done something that had him thrown in prison. So Donna stayed with her husband, but of course, he continued the cycle of cheating, because it was just to easy for him.

A lot of women would throw themselves at him wherever he went, to the drugstore, or grocery store. Some women would always pay attention to him. So after about another four to five years of the infidelities by her husband, she finally did something. Donna begin to feel the need to pay her husband back. But what Donna did not realize is that this guy that she had been sharing her problems with at work, was now going to begin to manipulate her. Because this guy was married too, but he knew Donna was going through some things. He begin to create some stories about problems in his marriage. It worked like a charm!

Donna and her new manipulator begin to start sneaking around after work. Sometimes they would both call in on the same day and spend the entire day with each other. Then they would go home like they had been at work all day. This guy never intended on leaving his wife. But Donna thought so, because he had insinuated that he would leave his wife if the right circumstance came about. So Donna continued to pursue this married man at work.

There was this other married man at Donna's job that she really respected. That man asked Donna why is she doing what she is doing with another woman's husband. Donna told that man that another woman did her like that, so she does not care about his wife. Donna had become very bitter due to her husband, but she held women in general more responsible for her husband's cheating. Because after all, her aunts had gotten Donna conditioned to the idea that men will be men. Meaning that they will cheat eventually. So Donna now see herself in competition with all women. So if she has to step on another woman to get the man that she wants, then she does not have a problem with it!

So she pursued and pursued the married man that she worked with, to the point that when the married man became worried that his wife was going to find out, he requested to be transferred to another office, so that he did not have to come up with excuses no more. Donna believed his reasons though for transferring. He told her it would make it easier for his babysitting needs. Donna, of course, believed him.

Donna had developed this thing where she only would hear what she wanted to hear, and if it was not what she wanted to hear, then she would change the subject. Often, whenever someone said something to Donna agreeing with what she was doing or how she was living, Donna would draw close to them.

Now that the married man had transferred to another office and did not leave his wife, Donna begin to search for another man. Donna after cheating on her husband for awhile, gained the confidence to leave him. She put her husband out. Her husband knew it was coming because they had stopped having sex for awhile. He would want to and Donna would not let him. The husband fussed a little, but he figured that she just needed some time so he went ahead and moved out, figuring she would eventually call him back. Now Donna begin looking for another man because as Donna describes herself, she is a Self-professed Nympho! Meaning that she has to have sex, and often.

The bad thing is that she went on the internet to find her next manipulative relationship. She met this guy that had recently been released from spending time in prison. One thing all women should know about men that have spent time in prison, is that they get Ph.D.'s in manipulation in prison. That is the way they survive in prison. That is the way they get things in prison. So when they come out of prison with a felony on their record, unable to do much because of the felony, they will resort to what worked for them in prison. Manipulation!

Now Donna is corresponding with this guy on the internet. Right away he wants to make her at ease by telling her something he did not have to tell her. He tells her that he has a girlfriend, but he suspects that she has been cheating on him for awhile now. So right away Donna gave him her full trust because she felt like, he did not have to tell her that.

He went on to tell Donna that he was going to break it off with his girlfriend now that he found her. So they corresponded via the internet for a month before they finally met face-to-face. By that time he told Donna that he had broke up with his girlfriend, and that she was very upset. He even told Donna that his girlfriend said that she knew it was because of another woman, and she want to know who Donna was. Strangely, this made Donna excited.

When they finally met face-to-face, they had sex within a few hours of meeting up. Donna went to work bragging that he was the best she had ever had sex with, and she bragged that he was so well endowed that she could barely handle being with him. Donna actually told him, so now he knew he could do whatever, and even if he get caught, Donna would still be with him.

You remember that girlfriend he was suppose to have broken up with? Well, guess what happen! This guys birthday was coming up in a week. He was suppose to be calling Donna to let her know what time. Donna waited and waited, but no phone call came through to tell her what time his birthday party was going to be. You see, he lived 200 miles away so it was not like she could just jump in the car and take a ten minute drive to his house.

Donna finally called his mother's house, and she told her where and what time. When this guy got wind that his mother had told Donna, he immediately called Donna. He told Donna that his ex had got invited by his family, and she is going to have friends there. He then begin to manipulate Donna, by telling her that he just do not want his ex, and her girlfriends to try to fight her. Donna argued that should be her choice, but Donna finally let it go. But the showdown finally came.

Another month had went by, where Donna and this guy was traveling back and forth. Of course, this guy would have last minute cancellations many times. Well, one day Donna gets a phone call from a woman that she does not know, on this guy's phone. Donna asked her why are you calling me on his phone?! The woman responded because this is my boyfriend, and we live together. Donna then said, "Well he has been seeing me for two months now." The other woman said, "You can have him." But in the background, you could hear the guy begging his live-in girlfriend to stay, and telling her how much he wanted her. Donna was so hurt! But of course, this guy called back two days later and talked Donna into staying.

His excuse was that he did not have no where else to live, and he did not want to live with his momma. But the other woman called Donna after about a week and ask Donna what was she going to do, because she was still going to be with him. Donna told her that she was still going to be with him too. You see how manipulation works!

Both Donna and the other woman continued to be with this guy. But of course, time will tell the truth! After being with this guy for awhile, Donna began to see some warning signs about this guy. It turns out that as long as he does not drink alcohol, he was everything Donna wanted. But what Donna did not know because he hid it from her, was that he is an alcoholic.

Every time he takes her out to have a good time, it always gets ruined by his drinking.

When he drinks he becomes paranoid and insecure. He begins to think that every man in the spot is after Donna, or that Donna is looking at other men. This happens on a weekly basis. They argue all the time about his drinking. At the time this book was written, Donna and this guy was still together.

In order for Donna's life to get better, she is going to have to get rid of the idea that men are going to eventually cheat anyway. She is also going to have to change the type of men that she is drawn to. She is going to have to expect better from men. If the man cannot be trusted, stop helping him come up with excuses. She have to

stop excepting betrayals like it is just a part of

life.

CHAPTER SEVEN

MICHELLE

Michelle is a woman that long for attention. Michelle at a young age had an accident where she had gotten burned on her chest. As she grew up she underwent a lot of teasing from other kids that she went to school with. As she grew up she healed and the scars kind of faded. As Michelle became older, she began to over compensate as a defense mechanism.

Michelle got married at a young age. Her husband was very dominating. He was a jealous man. He would always get upset if she would just say, "Hello" to someone. Michelle would comply to her husband because she knew no other way. After Michelle finally left her husband because of his cheating, Michelle realized that she had been living in a situation like a prison. In fact, Michelle told me that now being out of the situation, she can see how she was living like she had been sentenced to prison. Also, Michelle said that everything was about what he wanted.

Her husband really did not care what she wanted or desired. But because Michelle had gone through this experience in her life, Michelle came to the conclusion that she would never conform to traditional societal ideals of relations again. Also, Michelle decided that since other women had slept with her husband, that she would not have respect for any other women. Michelle now made it her aim to pay back all women for what a few other women had done to her.

I came to know Michelle at a company where we both worked. Michelle had been putting word out that she wanted to have sex with me. I did not know for awhile, but a couple of guys at the job came to me and asked have I heard what was going around. The two guys told me that Michelle is telling everyone that she is feeling me! She is telling people that she is going to have her way with you!

I told them that I am married. They replied, she said she love married men. They then said every time you walk by she is watching you and saying stuff. I then told them, well it's not going to happen! Of course, both of the guys did not believe me because at that company there was a lot of people doing things they should not have been doing from the top of the company, to the bottom.

Michelle finally began to make advances

toward me. I ignored her thinking she would see that I was not interested in her and move on, but it seem like the more I ignored her, the more determined she became, to try and conquer me. It got to the point where she became so desperate to try to get me to sleep with her, that she began to insult me subtlety, by saying that I was not a man in so many words. So I told her that if Lisa Ray and Beyonce can't make me cheat, than she definitely was not going to be able to! This young girl then proceeded to ask me, is it that serious? I then told her if you ever got something real in your life, then you will see how serious it is.

In a way I kind of felt sorry for her, because she really had no clue! I even tried to help her to understand that she should not want a man that can only give her part of his time, but she should want a man that can give her all of his time. Michelle told me that I appreciate what you are trying to do, but I am not trying to hear that. So I told Michelle, No! No! No! It's not going to happen. Michelle then said, "Okay, I will leave you alone, but if you ever change your mind, you always can. Michelle soon left the company and I have not seen her since.

CHAPTER EIGHT

PAM

Pam is a young lady that never knew her father. This is because Pam's mother was rumored to be a prostitute. So Pam's mother has no idea who Pam's father is. Pam was taken away from her mother at a young age. Pam grew up in foster homes, and group homes. Although group homes, are better than living on the street, it does not replace the nurturing that comes from being in a loving home with both parents.

Pam grew up finding herself drawn to dominating, borderline abusive males. Pam told me one time that if a guy is just too in to her, and too nice to her, she gets board with them quickly. If she will even give them the time of day. Also, Pam told me that if a guy treats her like she does not exist, it is something about that, that draws her to that guy.

Pam has older sisters and an older brother, but they are no help, when it comes to giving sound advice. Pam's family are actually a drain on her. They have caused her to get kicked out of an apartment.

Pam talks to me on a regular basis, because she looks at me like a father. In fact, she sends me Father Day cards yearly. When we talk, however, Pam tends to avoid topics or ignore topics that she does not want to deal with. Because when we talk, it is like a real father and daughter relationship. So sometimes I have to say things to Pam that she does not like, but it is out of concern for her welfare that I do it.

Pam tried being in a relationship with a nice guy, but it did not last. Pam cannot explain it, but she did not feel the desire to be with this guy. She admits that he was good to her, but she still did not feel a connection to him. Pam continues to be drawn to the guy she had her son by, that happens to be locked up in prison. The guy that as she said, treated her like she did not exist.

So Pam continues to be in a continuing cycle. The problem is that the guys that Pam is attracted to, are not acting like they do not care about her. They really do not care about her. After those guys get what they want from her, they will move on, or they will be with other women, and keep Pam on the side. Either way, it is a dangerous relationship to be in.

CHAPTER NINE

<u>TRACY</u>

Tracy is a woman that craves a lot of attention. Also, Tracy is a woman that has very low self-esteem. Tracy is always seeking validation. Although Tracy is married, she is always seeking the attention of other men. Tracy for some reason or another needs the validation, of other men.

It seems that if another man carries on like he wants Tracy sexually, she feels validated. A lot of women seem to need that validation from other men. It is as if the man that they're with is lying or something, when he tells her that she looks good, or is beautiful. This might not be so bad, but it has been rumored that Tracy has actually acted on some of the advances that have come her way from some men.

Tracy's husband works very hard and does a pretty good job taking care of the family financially, but Tracy's husband has never been a person that connects with people emotionally. Tracy knew that, before she married him. Tracy, however, thought she could change him. Well, it did not work, but over the years while trying to change her husband, she played dangerous games. Tracy would do things on purpose to try and make her husband jealous, and to try and control him. Tracy had seen this work for another woman that Tracy looked up to. Tracy has always been a follower. In fact, Tracy would literally try to become other people that she seen on TV, or in the community.

Tracy began to do things like when her and her husband went out, she would purposely stand away from her husband, to give other men the idea that she was there alone. Of course, men would try to hit on her. Tracy did this often, and then would act as if she was not doing anything. Any relationship where someone in the couple feels they need to resort to behavior like this, is extremely unhealthy.

Tracy complains all the time that she does not know if her husband loves her. Well, after going through the games that Tracy played on him, maybe he conditioned himself to not show any emotions. Just so he can be able to keep his sanity. Tracy's husband, however, complains that Tracy does not appreciate anything. He has given her a lot materially - houses, cars and regular vacation trips.

If any relationship proves that money will not make you happy, it is this one. Tracy's husband has earned over $150,000 a year for several years now, and they have been more unhappy, than happy. The sad thing is that they are still together, and it has been rumored that Tracy has had several affairs behind her husband's back. Also, Tracy feels that her husband is cheating on her, but that could just be because, she is trying to justify to herself that she had a right to cheat, or it could very well be true. Everyone has a breaking point if they feel they are not being respected, and treated right.

CHAPTER TEN

<u>MARY</u>

Mary is a woman that comes from a large family. Mary grew up in a family that underwent a lot of turmoil, tension and stress. So over the years, Mary became conditioned to except unforeseen events or situations that may arise in her life. Mary's mother and father got divorce while Mary was still young. Mary witnessed a very bad divorce.

Also, Mary witnessed her father be broken by the divorce. Mary remembers her father wanting to stay in the home until she and her siblings got older. Mary remembers how mean her mother treated her father. Mary's mother would not agree to let Mary's father stay in the house, to see his children grow up. Mary could not understand what could change that much, to make her mother hate her father like this all of a sudden!

But shortly after, Mary's father moved out, another man that Mary did not know, and had never seen before, moved in with Mary's family. Mary's mother had married another man. This man was no where the character of a man that Mary's father was, and Mary was forced to live through this situation. Mary had just barely had to deal with the splitting up of her mother and father.

Now Mary had to live in a house with a stranger. Not only a stepfather, but also a stepbrother that was not very nice to Mary. That is a hard situation for a young lady to have to deal with, in such a short transition period. Mary had to survive emotionally. This would have a life long effect on Mary.

You see Mary's mother never ever thought about the affects on her children. Mary's mother only thought about what she wanted, and needed. Most parents put the needs of their children first, but not Mary's mother. You see Mary's mother had not been raised by her mother, and that affected her for life. Mary's mother grew up without the love and nurturing of her birth mother. She had no understanding of how a mother is suppose to be toward her children. She lacks compassion, and the ability for compassion.

Mary's mother grew up learning how to survive by any means necessary. That is the only skill she ever developed. So Mary's mother only was able to give her children what she knew. Mary had to grow up in a house that she really did not want to be in, but had no choice. Mary was only taught how to work.

From an early age, Mary's mother found Mary a job. Mary has been working since she was 12 years old. However, Mary was not able to keep her money. Mary's mother took most of it. This continued into Mary's adult life. Mary was very attached to her mother, and did not want to do anything to displease her mother for many years. The sad thing is, that Mary's mother lacked any real connection to Mary. Mary was her mothers meal ticket.

As a young adult, Mary was paying most of

the bills in the house, and buying needed items for her younger siblings. Mary's mother did not work. So the only skill that Mary's mother had, was to survive by any means necessary. She was surviving off of Mary. Mary's mother is so self-absorbed, that Mary was unable to save money to get her own place to live. Mary's mother was making sure that she took more than half of Mary's money, to pay all the bills in the house.

One day, this guy came along that had always liked Mary. By chance, this guy asked Mary if she would like to hang out for the day. Mary agreed to meet this guy, at the mall. So they met at the mall and did some window shopping. Mary and the guy sat and talked at the food court. After talking for awhile this guy had been liking Mary since the fourth grade, and did not want to give any other guys a chance to step in. So he asked Mary if she would like to be boyfriend and girlfriend. Mary really wanted a boyfriend, so she said yes.

At first, everything was cool with Mary's family because they did not think Mary's new relationship, was that serious. But after awhile when Mary's mother realized that Mary was really in love with this guy, Mary's mother and family started to try and discourage Mary from being with her boyfriend. Mary's older brother went to her boyfriend's father, and told him that their family were wanting someone better for Mary. Her family did not care what Mary wanted.

The funny thing is that, her older brother ended up divorced from his wife. He cheated on her several times, but Mary's family was good at trying to give advice, when they were failures in relationships. None of them had learned how to love, how to give of themselves to another person, and how to make another person happy.

All they learned was selfishness.

Mary's older sister, even tried to advise Mary, to get to know other men. Before she decides to settle with this guy. Mary's older sister, ended up having two divorces. Well, the good thing is that Mary, grew up paying attention to her family mistakes. Mary recognized, the hypocrisy in her family. Mary did not want to make the same mistakes as her family.

This guy really loved Mary, and she could feel it. So Mary did not listen to her family. Mary ended up marrying this guy. Mary has been married now for over 20 years, and have had much more happier times, than sad ones. Mary loves her husband and is so happy that she made up her own mind, to be with her husband.

Mary continues to work on herself everyday, because she wants to be the best wife, lover and friend, she can be to her husband. The reason Mary was able to over come the pitfalls of her family, is because she wants to do right. She wants to be honest with herself. She want to recognize, what she needs to work on. She wants to work on them.

Mary's willingness, has saved her. Because

Mary has to work hard to keep her family tendencies, from creeping into her life. Because her family has a tendency to get angry, whenever they are wrong. They will not admit they're wrong. But Mary is always working to grow. Once again it is her willingness, that have saved her from failure. The fact that she has a good man, has helped her as well. A man, that loves her. Love, conquers all. Love does not give up!

A GOOD MAN!

A good man will care about what you want, and desire!

A good man will encourage you!

A good man will look for your positives!

A good man will make you known, even when you are not around, or with him!

A good man will not overstate your mistakes!

A good man will not leave you behind, even when you tell him it's okay to go!

A good man will always give you his best effort!

A good man will always be ready to defend you!

CONCLUSION

This book was in no way meant to be malicious towards anyone. This book was written for the purpose of showing how some women have been trained for failure. Because some women grow up looking to be taken care of, but never work on developing there worth, or value. That's why so many women get used, and taken advantage of. Because no matter how bad it is, there will always be some men, that use what they have, or what they appear to have materially, to take advantage of women that are seeking a man for material possessions.

There is not only mothers training their daughters in this manner. There is fathers training their daughters in this manner. There have been some fathers that have not allowed their daughters to talk to some young men, that do not have a lot accomplished materially. No matter how much he knows his daughter cares about the young man.

A lot of young women have gone onto marry young men that their fathers, were attracted too. Their fathers feel are the best possible providers. Often how the young man is going to treat his daughter, is often overlooked.

So many times the young man that does have a lot of possessions, ends up looking at the young lady as another one of his possessions. Often he will treat her as if he could take her, or leave her. He often tries to make her feel like she should feel fortunate, that he chose her. He will even sometimes go as far as to, constantly reminding her of how many other women, wants him.

Every once in awhile you will hear of a young man that has accomplished things materially, and are good people, but not too often. There are so many things a young lady opens herself up to, when she is trained to look for a materially advantaged mate. Manipulation, disloyalty, verbal and physical abuse, betrayal and many other negatives. All too often young ladies get unsolicited advice from women that have made a lot of mistakes, and continue to make mistakes. How can a failure teach you how to be a winner? They cannot!

So ladies if you want to know how to be successful in relationships, than you need to talk to women that have long successful relationships. Do not believe that everyone that are in successful relationships are settling. Because that is what failures would like you to believe. That everyone that is in a long lasting relationship, is just settling. There are some happy people that have been married for many years!

The points of this book is also to drive home the point, that there are warning signs that need to be paid attention to. There are some warning signs that just scream out stop!!! Do not past go, run the other way, as fast as you can!

Also, one of the most important points in the book is for women to expect better for themselves and not allow other women that are stuck in a cycle, to convince you that it is just the way things are. That you are going to just have to except some bad behavior. No! No! No! If you do not expect better for yourself, you will never get it. The definition of insanity is, to continue to do the same thing, and expect a different result. So if you want to change your life around, you must do something different. Change your views, change your approach, and change the way you think. Retrain yourself. Shed the training you received growing up. The training, that is making you fail!